FOOLS' PARADISE

FOOLS' PARADISE

GREVEL LINDOP

CARCANET/MANCHESTER

Some of these poems have appeared in the following periodicals, to whose editors acknowledgement is made: *Box, Carcanet, Caret, Critical Quarterly, Isis, Pause, PN Review, Poetry Nation,* and *Tagus*. Some were broadcast by BBC Radio 3 in 'Poetry Now', and a number appeared in *Poetry Introduction II*, Faber & Faber, 1972; and in *Ten English Poets*, Carcanet, 1976. Some first appeared in the pamphlet *Against the Sea*, Carcanet, 1970.

Thanks also to Keith Munnings, for help in finding the dust-jacket illustration.

SBN 85635 215 2

Copyright © Grevel Lindop 1977

All Rights Reserved

First published in 1977
by Carcanet New Press Limited
in association with Carcanet Press Limited
330 Corn Exchange Buildings
Manchester M4 3BG

Printed in Great Britain by Unwin Brothers Ltd.
at the Gresham Press, Old Woking, Surrey

Lear: Dost thou call me fool, boy?
Fool: All thy other titles thou hast given away; that thou wast born with.
— *Shakespeare*

If the fool would persist in his folly, he would become wise.
— *Blake*

FOR RACHEL

CONTENTS

- 9   Fools' Paradise
- 10   Spot-Welder's Song
- 11   Buying Valentines
- 12   The Hands
- 13   Noon at Bursa
- 14   The Place
- 15   The Tell-tale Heart
- 16   Charlie on Death Row
- 17   The Tattooist
- 18   The Truth about Ariadne
- 19   Ovid in Exile
- 20   Bluebeard's Wife
- 21   Caption
- 22   The Barrel-Dance
- 23   Ampersand
- 24   The Landlord
- 25   The Core
- 26   Mirror and Candle
- 27   Philosopher
- 28   Legend
- 29   Cornish Tin Mine
- 30   Entropy
- 31   Under the Clock
- 32   Seven Love-Poems
- 39   Valuable Building-Plot for Sale
- 40   Horses in Rain
- 42   Shropshire Union Canal
- 43   Winter Poem for Osip Mandelstam
- 44   A Letter from Provence
- 45   The Sophist
- 46   Joseph's Coat
- 47   Fish-Shop
- 48   Purposes of a Poem
- 50   Sleeper
- 51   Perplexed by the Sunlight
- 52   A Falling House
- 53   Colour Words

54 Interface
55 Condemned Houses
56 Ophelia at her Mirror, Undecided
57 Dictionary
58 The Horoscope
59 Mirrors
60 Playing the Fruit-Machine
61 The Vampire's Confession
62 Sade in Prison
63 The Island
64 Moving

FOOLS' PARADISE

The only paradise is Fools' Paradise,
all sane men know—
a land grown fertile on strata
of wish, dream, metaphor
and rivers of legend that persist
under the mountains of logical ice
where Descartes shivers with his 'cogito'
wrapped round him, sure of his own mind but no
whit warmer in a world he cannot trust.

Still we set out again on our fools' quest,
seeking a country where the rules
are different, where the wise
go mad with common sense
and round the fires
of love and revolution all the fools
pull off their rags and laugh to see the king
stripped of his laws and all his train of soldiers,
naked and in his right mind again.

We are content to be the lunatics
for now. Under the glacier, rivers grow
towards a flood, and while the lion Marx
roars at the city gates
the wise ones in the palace chatter on,
piling philosophies like empty glasses
and tolerating the fools for entertainment
as once, no doubt, they threw
small change to trumpeters in Jericho.

THE SPOT-WELDER'S SONG

My hand is a fist of metal,
distended limb of a cripple, slung
to the ceiling on chains and cables:
I grip the seam of this scarred hulk
in a clench like a steel finger and thumb
and the volts thud into the skirts
of this car-shell, jolt my steel clench
(its bloodless digits) numb.

My fingers are lost in their gauntlets,
my face asbestos, a cyclops-eye of mica.
I can touch nothing, nor see with a naked eye:
only the metal is naked, that spreads
under the hands I shift, and takes
each blow and burning into itself like love
or purgatory, calmly,
so it can move out scarlet or clean green
slick as a mirror in every cellulosed limb
sealed of the scars from my ham-fisted forge.

And down the chain-striped halls
components go by like hunks of meat on hooks
chained too. That insect-progress carries them
and soothes the circuits of the brain
until the hands climb their own course,
swing up the welding-gun again
(the hinge and rivet know it all)
grip to a seam and in my arc
fire more blind power from its source.

And you, wired harem bride for the iron Pharoah,
new model for the sad man's lust,
love for you, if there is love, 'll be
somewhere else:
we hammer you because we must,
flat-heart machine, frog-faced queen,
hungry rust.

BUYING VALENTINES

Months can surprise us: today,
for instance, cold February holds
so many aces in her hand:
the shops blush and billow with hearts,

vermilion, cherry and lavender hearts,
all colours of the candy-spectrum—
even a few in lace. A chorus
of little whores, singing of how

you can earn love, or buy, it will be like this:
a calendar-full of lipstick kisses,
sweet hearts that open for your inspection,
a mere date making a new mistress.

And February always brings them:
these mental hearts refuse to perish,
or rather they come back yearly like leaves
unfolding in their own season

and we buy them, thinking it's a year
since last we bought such innocence,
glad no one will open them unwillingly
unlike letters or telegrams,
or other cards the months deal out.

THE HANDS

Busy and blindfold, taught their trade by trial
and touch, they are naturals, eager exponents
of every half-formed thought, or of no thought.
Getting bored, they twiddle their thumbs or tap,
thinking that you are thinking nothing,
waiting to run an errand to pen or pocket.

The devil, they say, finds work for idle hands.
Idle heads will build their own contraptions
but wreak no havoc till hands are called to service:
hands in hatred of hands hammered iron
nails into the palms, twisted a crown,
offered the dice their chance to make decision.

The pride of heads denies them understanding
then reaches out a hand to prove the world,
explain its music and articulate
precise intelligence of love. The dark,
the silent, all comply to the hand's order,
make their confession to the finger tips

as honest as those bluntly-put inquiries.
No artists, they'll create by mere assuming
as they assume you now, love, substance you
out of the night's negations. Magic of touch,
you're there again. I feel you reach towards me.
The darkness round us sings the praise of hands.

NOON AT BURSA

This is a loveless time. Outside,
old women rest the ache of years
under an olive-tree;
their heavy thoughts move in the sand.

All things withdraw
but heat, and a few shadows,
and what makes no resistance to the light.

My hotel room has paled
and stripped to the persuasive sun
for years: surviving
so many ages of wrinkled black
by sheer defiance, nakedness
of the bone, not the skin:
white overseer to lives that dry like grapes.

And conscious of the shade of love,
I am obscurely shamed by those women
in their loveless time, all things
withdrawn, hungry for shadows.

Bursa, Turkey; September 1969

THE PLACE

There was a meeting: sometime. But the place
remains, for them, the constant. The dry
fountain with its dusty stone throat;
the point where buses stopped, anticipating
olive-traders from the market; the café.

Before this place came a chance encounter,
after it refuge in the hotel; a
delayed embrace; the solitude of dressing;
making the bed together, silent. All
less sharp, now, than the lemon sunlight
of the place caught in that marble cup
and remembered; or, perhaps, imagined.

THE TELL-TALE HEART

No need to tell how long he had endured
the old man's raving. It seemed at last he must have
grown thoroughly inured.

He would sit up, when ordered, half the night;
would check the tyrant's figures, copy his cramped notes
by meagre candlelight.

Charged with deceit or sloth, he gave no sign
of anger, fingers steady on the account-book
ruling the black line

with never a smudge of sweat. At most, by chance
catching the maid's eye, he would enlist her
sympathy with a glance.

A single murmur would have meant the sack.
Who knows what senile snarl, what final flung word
broke this poor drudge's back?

He spent this morning by the lake. Somehow
small pressures build: he walks at last with firm tread
back to the house. And now,

some slowly-growing want at last obeyed,
carefully he unlocks the desk drawer,
pensively thumbs the blade.

CHARLIE ON DEATH ROW

Look at your heart and you see a newspaper clipping.
Someone translates your speech for you,
you get your blood from the bank.
Your midnights yawn, your noon's gone out to lunch.
Sure you can come and look.
What do you see? I think the doctors
drained the colours from your mind's eye at birth.

Your head's shut in with a skull:
they riveted it on,
screwed a metal cap to your brain.
Now you're segmented as an insect. Your limbs
would pull off, one, two, three,
a talking head and a brittle ticking thorax.
You think our blood can be lost,
think you can waste us
and rub your hands to wipe the poison off?

You think a dismantling is a death,
and you fear death. Come closer,
he's sitting on my shoulder.
Still you demand the 'Supreme Penalty'.
I can see crowds of people shuffling the street.
They sniff at newspapers
to get a hit off the execution headlines.

THE TATTOOIST

She asked me for a butterfly
there, on her shoulder. No one knows
what goes on under the skin.
I was a man with time to kill
for money, and an art to sell,
patient enough with my line
to take the minimum of pain
filling a chosen space
and never choosing the design.

I worked at a square inch,
a needle nuzzling the skin.
I wiped the blood off where the line
was drawn, a blue embroidery
in the margin of her world.
She paid, and I am free to stay
like the icecream man and the clairvoyante
and the others who sell their addictions,
and she goes wrapped in the new web of her body:
she will never be naked again.

THE TRUTH ABOUT ARIADNE

No wonder Theseus fled the island
leaving her there to die upon the sand,
her body torn by his child's life:
how else could he have exorcized the memory
of her dark face, and those small hands
holding the twine to thread the labyrinth?

And turning his love to shame, in his heart
remained the memory that after fighting
his way to the central chamber of the maze,
blood on his hands, the monster dead behind him,
he found her there, laughing in triumph, proud
to greet him, now her spells were all unwound.

Theseus, whose love was strictly the benign
effulgence of male pride, turning misogynist
took his revenge on woman-kind
(Helen, Persephone, the Amazons)
and saw in each what he most feared to see:
the mocking face of his wild-haired Ariadne—

whilst she, on Naxos, lay with Dionysus
(who, as a god, was used to travel light
and had no use for memory, or pride).

OVID IN EXILE

At the outposts of a broken language
I have lived lately. These barbaric provinces:
the worst wine in the empire, no books, and the most
execrable climate. (I have a few notes of
such grammar as persists here, having to instruct
my servants. His Imperial Highness would not
be interested.) A poem will not suffice
for this bone-grasping cold, let alone
death, or loneliness. Like the provincials,
such things would need physical violence
to make them intelligible. The grunts
of these oxen express them more accurately.

As for you, Julia, if you expect a poem,
you can go to the Emperor and let him
fondle you with his greasy hexameters.

More real than any poem I can make
are the dreams of you that shake me
nightly, and wring me dry, body and mind.

And these I cannot send you, my dearest.

BLUEBEARD'S WIFE

Like Alice, I stepped into a cool mirror
to a place where the clock had a smiling face,
to a garden of talking flowers:
but when I walked the gravel paths to meet you
began the game of hide and seek and
further you withdrew at every step
(O master of the primal mansion), further,
to tower over the trembling land
like a mirage of God on the sky, and all the while
a bunch of keys sang 'Bluebeard' in your hand,

'Bluebeard', they whispered, and the more I loved,
more I was drawn into the dark of eyes'
fathomless pupils, drowning,
swimming down until something was solid inside.
Like a small fish I curled at night
warm on a pulsing pillow,
dreaming in the red chambers of a heart
(I couldn't tell if yours or mine),
the soft walls soothing as they surged apart

then closed again. I was a child exploring:
rooms opened into rooms, and in my hand
the keys sang at each door and charmed the lock;
rooms of the throat, the skin, the womb
unfolded, offered themselves to me,
and still I was alone until the last
door opened and I found you small and face
to face, staring at me as at a glass.
I touched you, but you didn't notice.
Now I shall leave the house and set you free.

CAPTION

Photograph of a corner-shop, its rust-red
paintwork framing a collage of gaudy
adverts, *Brook Bond Tea, Senior
Service Satisfy, Tizer, Park Drive*
on the windows, and the interior beyond
cool blue-green like an aquarium.
A hoop-backed upright chair on the paving-stones
recalls the old woman who sat like a doll
there one hot day, eyes closed to the light,
thin wrists composed on knees, completing
my picture, I thought, until I returned
with a camera and she was gone,
just the chair keeping its spindly shadow
at the edge of the stone doorstep.
   Park Street or Albert Street, one of the places
you couldn't find now under the rubble
of demolition and the cleared earth even
with a map, any more than now
I could trace to some junk-shop that cheap
wooden chair which waits in the photograph,
stage left, the seat still cool in the sun
for someone
who in a moment will step again
into the street and rest there.

THE BARREL-DANCE

For a year I lived over a pub.
Monday and Wednesday mornings
I worked with half a mind, my ear
attuned to the traffic's rumblings
in the street, awaiting the warm beat
of an engine idling below:
the brewery wagon. When it came,
the world opened and I was at the window
to watch the new barrels unloaded—
not your spry aluminium kegs
but all the dead weight of iron hoop and wood
stave, and about nine gallons of beer:
a weight that if one of them took
a sudden drop could crush a man's foot
and crack the paving-stone under it.

The driver would climb up over
the tailboard, sing out for the landlord
and then with a roll and a toss
spring the first barrel over the side
of the wagon and down to his mate
who'd catch it as it fell
with a thud that shook the building
on a coconut-fibre pad at his feet,
and spinning the cask on one rim
skate it towards the cellar
like a weightless dancing-partner
and juggle it horizontal to roll down the chute.

I thought no dancer or acrobat
could match the rhythm of their work,
their art of weight and movement,
but like all performing artists
they improved the world not a jot:
I never drank in the pub,
for the landlord remained a churl
and the beer in his glasses warm and flat.

AMPERSAND

'And *per se* and', the grammarians,
the stammering pedants, christened you at first;
but at your usual short-cut game
you slipped a syllable, old escapist,
to come out like a clown with a clown's name.

I remember you in black on primrose,
twenty-seventh in my Edwardian alphabet-book,
drawn as a snake tied in a knot with a grin
on its face, which pleased me more than the innocent
B-for-Baker or S-for-Sailorman.

I find you like an outlaw in other guises:
rampant in gold on book-jackets as
a back-to-front 3 with a foot in the air;
or scrawled like a plus-sign by people who
don't know what you're called and don't care;

but that's all right. You'll cross any frontier
in Europe. Convenience will see you through.
Typeface jester, strange hunchback,
camp-follower of the alphabet,
our laziness & haste rely on you.

THE LANDLORD

The landlord turns in his sleep, hearing a footfall
somewhere on a stair,
deep in the spiralled hollows of his ear.
His heart returns like a pendulum in the dark.

Mentally, mentally he inspects the attic:
his dreams are hung like dustsheets on a chair,
his keys are hanging on a nail,
the dust hangs in the air.
Nobody has been trespassing there.

All's well. He considers now the cupboards,
makes inventory of small things
of which only he is aware:
electric plugs, a dusty sponge, a hundred newspapers
shed from the forests of the wooden year—

each in its place. His inward eye
returns to rest. But we must move carefully,
avoid the creaking boards, speak in a whisper,
not to disturb this ghost who dreams the house.

I imagine him sleeping up there, making his bed
perhaps in a trunk or a clock-case,
where agile mice play havoc with his moustache
around the roaring caverns of his nostrils.

Don't laugh, don't make a sound; or he might wake,
shake off his dream, send the floorboards tilting,
the windows crashing, the cellars caving under him,
and shake us too awake, to find ourselves
without shelter and free on the cold ground.

THE CORE

Cut through an apple and you find a star.
There is a mathematics of design
and symbol in the artifice of nature:
the fall that shook the fruit from Newton's tree
pulls down the meteor, and for a sign
the apple keeps its hidden signature,
an asterisk embedded in the heart
referring to a single symmetry
beyond the laws that cut the world apart.

MIRROR AND CANDLE

The mirror and the candle throw
their incantation through the room
and on the wall our shadows loom
monstrous in their reverberate glow.

Their occult transformations make
our bed a range of hills, the floor
a flickering plain edged with the shore
that borders on a glassy lake.

We act our legends in that space.
The mirror takes, the candle gives,
and light from both the eye receives
to conjure out that doubled place

where through the sky our shadows pass
drowned in the depths that wait below.
I rest my cheek on the pillow
and in the fathoms of the glass

you reach across the dark to me.
The light flows back the way it came.
High on its tower of wax the flame
sings songs of mutability.

PHILOSOPHER

Restless in the evening,
he took paper boats
and set them sailing
from the shore of his thoughts,
watching them a little after
they passed out of sight.

LEGEND

You are walking through a forest.
You are a girl with long yellow hair
and a ruby pinned at your breast.

You pass under an oak-tree
and a small bird drops from the branches to swoop
and snatch your jewel away,

and the pin gashes you;
you lift your fingers to the place
and the red blood runs through,

runs through, and runs, and last of all
a small bird struggles from the wound
and flies up with a high-pitched call

and now you haunt the tops of trees
watching the path for the next girl,
envious, hungry for rubies.

CORNISH TIN MINE

You might think it grew, a tor
vegetating from the clogged
desiccated upland soil:
if stone took organic form
to fight the wind, it would be
like this, half shell half boulder.

This is not so. Walk closer
and the living signs of work
are clear: chewed by rain and wind
chimney and engine-house show
the cell-pattern of mortar,
the patient structuring of

men who handled every stone
single, like a loaf of bread,
learning its bulk with their hands,
placing it to interlock
shape and weight with each neighbour.
It must have taken great care

and great skill. They did it well
for what that's worth. The vein's dry,
those hard scraped palms and short nails
gone. Only some families
round here once ate from the mine,
dug weddings and clothes from it.

Now it's landscape or landmark
even to their grandchildren.
Nature pretends to own it.
But if God saw, he might be
cross at this clenched fist, index
finger pointed at the sky.

ENTROPY

is the running-down of a clock
where galaxies are cogs;
always, at last, the pattern
of vein or diatom or word
is broken. All resistance
sinks, the most subtle first.

Behind dead eyelids, disorder
increases: the crystalline lens
slacks its hold on possible light,
concepts crumble, protein cliffs
of memory erode without resistance.
All this in a few hours.

Omnivorous time at last
swallows itself, and then?

We camp on a whale's back;
the sea covers every island.
With what we are, we build
monuments against the sea.

UNDER THE CLOCK

Old man, stroke down your long white hair
again. The boy beside you sits
unmoved: his thoughts discard all you can say
now he has summed you, finally.

His beauty is insistent, yours
only a thin despairing charm
that sinks in gratitude to feel
his knee against your knee, your dry
humiliated hand beside his on a glass.

What can you say? You would kneel for him,
you would play woman to his hands,
you would give him money. And instead

you play the old man wise, pale-skinned,
drinking under the calm clock
that stirs the smoky air. The bar is quiet.
He leaves without a word. You stay, of course.
The tears of time tick on your face.

SEVEN LOVE-POEMS

1. *The Impossibility of Love-Poems*

To use a tape-recorder,
photographs, diaries—
would it be easier?
Still the impossibilities
lure me into
a hopeless endeavour:

to tell, somehow,
about your being
in body or in thought
or character. And though
you are my meaning,
what survives is something else:
colour-words, not colours;

particular shapes of thought
that carry your impress
faintly, like once-worn clothes,
are all I can keep.
I write about choosing words for you,
and the words choose what they express.

2. *Prelude*

Your first glance at the mirror
is always a surprise,
and cannot well be otherwise:

still drowsy at morning
you must replace
the daylight's mask against your face,

giving up dream's anonymous freedom,
content to be marked down
with flesh. No wonder if you frown,

finding it always different
from the face remembered
and still more from the face preferred,

and turn with some reserve to me,
remembering that I
have only this to know you by.

3. *Preferring Silence*

Over the crest of each knuckle
and under the bridge of a ring
run the blue veins that keep their course
across the landscape of your hand
as long as your heart agrees to sustain
their periodic ripple.

Sudden anger or fear
would be enough to alter
that smooth pace, one pulse to the second,
and love, of course, would do the same
since no heart takes pains to spare
these beats where our time is reckoned

but lets them run to waste,
spending what force it must
whether greeting lover or murderer,
like an ignorant bell that batters
alike for wedding or deathknell,
preferring silence to either.

4. *Too Much Care*

Able, in writing, to revise
any mistaken word or clumsy phrase,
we start to think: how much better
to write, than to meet face to face.
So writing becomes a shield; that is, a barrier.

Unable, in speech, to alter
things once said, we play for safety
now, say only what will bear repeating
and so shut out our hope of meaning—
the truth of gesture or emotion
too much care takes out, and can't replace.

5. *4 A.M.*

You will put me together again,
I know. Now my circuits are wrong,
I carry my heart on my wrist like a little red watch
and its movement is slow, the jerks
of my body are all that can shake its dull
springs into life. Soon it won't go

at all. Time is already folding
in on itself. I wake in the small hours
with both hands cramped, hurting so
as I flex them on fistfuls of dark, I imagine
the thin bird-bones showing through, hollowed
by pain to a thin X-ray glow.

I turn in a hard wilderness of sheets,
and somewhere the smooth earth turns its slow
cheek to the light, and white edges
unmirror the black window. That's
indifferent, no concern of mine,
until you come and make it so.

6. Before a Visit

The sky is empty. I'm with you at Euston
as you get on the night train, alone.
Mentally I watch waves of tired pigeons
spill against the glass vault of the station.

I time you. Now you're sitting opposite
some heavy man asleep in the compartment
trying to drink and hold your coffee still
and hold yourself still in the flying fragments

of dead light, the drumming rush of rail-connections,
the flickering chaos where your pale twin rides
left-handed, introvert, sad outside the glass,
separate from you like me: I sympathize,

I imagine us going down on those rails
in a tumble. The sleepers flash under our heads.
We'll hammer love like nails into the calendar.
Our hearts will wake the angels from their beds.

7. *Touch Wood*

I imagine your death,
and see it as a removal of weight and colour:
the spectrum washed away by rain,
a world seen through one mind
and all perspective gone
in the absence of double vision.

I should be light as paper
blow in the wind and cast no shadow,
a painted figure on pencil-lines of sky
mildly surprised to see the light
through my water-colour hand.
And the past acts of this figure?

What's real comes from your existence,
the chiaroscuro of solid things,
the dyes that crowd into the blankness of pure thought,
which alone is tasteless and colourless as Acid.

Pervade me still, longer,
let the colours of your mind
stain my world with inscape
that fire or flood, the cold of deaths or anger's
insane glitters can do nothing to change,

but stays like the dyes poured into molten glass
which become the glass itself,
soluble in no medium but glass,
inseparable, indifferent to breakage.

VALUABLE BUILDING-PLOT FOR SALE

The sundial is overthrown,
its finger broken, its head in the grass,
and the glass from the windows is gone.
Entering, I find the nave like a barn
where torn hymnbooks lie face down
on the flags like a massacre of pigeons.
The hassocks have grown a damp velvet of moss.
Someone has used part of a pew
to make a fire. There are rags and sodden ashes.
I am out of the simple world,
the building will not give up its habit of symbols.
The vestry reeks of urine and cheap sherry
and in the corner a tramp is huddled
who mutters as he rolls over in sleep
fending something off with a clenched fist,
cursing an unseen adversary.

HORSES IN RAIN

Horses in rain, wandering
during grey noon
below the coal-scars

move among shadows
their spare configuration
restlessly,

more tentative than clouds
drifting, steady,
against the faces

of the black pyramids fetched
and tipped from those scars.
The tips are handfuls,

cupped for a moment and spilled
beside the piled packages
of sheds, pithead, railway housing,

tied with powerline and cable.
Before them walk the horses.
A pit-wheel overlooks.

These, in movement, suggest
awareness of time. The rest,
immobile, has no language:

it is waste,
human carelessness or
the inorganic.

Like survivors of the mine,
these half-dozen
horses graze

between canal and railway,
islanded for the present
in a conditional peace.

Even in their quiet
movements, freedom's limits
are traced. Implied

like a well-known fence
is the unmoving fact:
the pit is background,

its tangles and pyramids never
more than a degree
away from eyesight.

SHROPSHIRE UNION CANAL

This unexpected night,
warmer by five degrees,
cleared the coal-heaps of white,
thawed out the iced-up quays

and unobtrusively
without a jolt or shock
set the canal-boats free
and opened every lock.

WINTER POEM FOR OSIP MANDELSTAM (1891-1938?)

I light a lamp by the white wall,
my breath steams in the empty rooms.
There was no warmth in your exile

but as I move in this cold house
to think of you seems natural
as making light in a dark place.

I remember how you refused to stop—
resting your paper on the lid of a suitcase,
writing poems while the stars sat up

(as you put it) like little bureaucrats
who watched you getting your world into shape
as they yawned over their nightly reports.

They buried you in their drifts of paper,
but under that snow of blanks your words
repeat themselves, a White Paternoster

to charm the blood back to its course
from all the internal wounds of Russia.
The rivers move under their ice:

the only strategy is persistence
in winter, to expect no sudden rescues
and wait for change in the slow seasons.

A LETTER FROM PROVENCE

Certainly, she has style.
From the envelope I shake out
a whole village: pink walls
spill together, the mountains settle
on my table, cypress-trees
straighten themselves among the clutter.

The church bell has a gummed back,
the main square is adorned
with a statue of France
cut from a postage-stamp.
The invitation to explore,
imagination
pursuing description through the bougainvillaea.

But someone is shooting a movie about anxiety
   (it is a movie, the neutrality of 'film'
   would be out of place,
   which has nothing to conceal or
   does not have to conceal a rather intrusive nothing
   which is felt where something should be)
and afterwards she will move on,
the location will change.

The village waits, indifferent,
to be folded, and I notice
it is on paper, catches no light,
no shadows either of sun or moon.

There is something
              I was expecting her to say.

THE SOPHIST

Let us deny
that lovers' vows
have no more worth
than fame allows:

the vows we seal
unbreakably
are *in*, not *for*
eternity.

Absolute truth
is not less sure
for knowing it
may not endure

when plunged into
the temporal mess:
not fact, but essence
words express.

But all the same
it's not a crime
to say that love's
the fool of time:

the master pays,
and as a rule
comes off less smartly
than the fool.

JOSEPH'S COAT

You wrap your body in the universe:
this is the many-coloured coat you wear
to keep you from the storm of nothingness.
No part can be left naked: to your eyes
the sky is sealed, your feet fill out the ground,
all air and water are the skin's draperies.
Move if you like. The coat moves with you:
new faces are embroidered on your blindfold,
it changes colour, but it stays and stays.
(Sleep is not nakedness but mere abeyance:
the dreamer's freedom is to recombine
new pictures from the patterns on his blanket.)
When you go down the pit, the coat survives.
Your brothers wear it. They don't mind the stains,
you signed the bargain when you put it on;
for wearing worlds, the price is known to be
an abstract Egypt of nonentity.

FISH-SHOP

We wait in the fish smell;
an aura of edible decay,
or of the too-fresh dead hooked and netted
and slapped here in heaps (apparently
still gasping for the sea)

and breathe the heavy oddity
of the fish. They look uncouth
as unborn souls snatched in embryo
out of their underworld womb.

The choice is rich (it's a Friday)—
the tinfoil mackerel, and plaice
daubed like buffoons with vermilion spots
and bruise-red mullet with salt on their suffering faces

wait in their masses. A hecatomb.
I feel utterly incomprehending.
What can you know about a fish?
It's arrogance even to eat them.

When I get to the counter it seems
more like some kind of drama.
The fish was a Christian symbol.
But these look glum and dully shocked

like the souls huddled at the wrong side
of a painted Last Judgement—
their eyes are like tawny coals, their mouths are slack

and a sign for frozen foods
on the salt-white tiling over them broods
like the Holy Ghost, an eagle lover,
a white bird by Braque.

PURPOSES OF A POEM

What shall I do with a poem?
I watch it detach itself
like a new beast from the background of blank jungle:
it's like inventing a word
when no one has used a word before
and no one knows what use the thing is
or knows how to say it's useless,
and I can't explain its use
without words, which are not yet invented
—or, perhaps, have been forgotten,
for time falls to pieces when,
where, there are no words,

and a poem is always the first
word in a new language
and time is always about to fall apart
or has just fallen apart and
is now coming together again into its ABC
orderly as the animals setting off for the ark,
a message in code for a new world,
and waiting to learn the new names
which the next Adam will offer them
after the blackboard of Babel has been washed clean
and the tongue is single again.

But the ark will never be reached: it has already sailed,
the forty days' deluge is permanently in mid-storm
and Noah is writing notes to put into bottles
at the eye of a maelstrom where 'just now'
and 'not yet' hurtle past, and causation turns seasick.

Yet a poem might reach him by paper-dart or pigeon
to tell him the animals are marching
and would answer their names if anyone cared
to call them; to tell him past and future
will not touch the ark and have not touched it

where it rests on top of the mountain of Now—
and that if he uncorks the bottle he is this moment
sealing, he will find already inside it
the poem I am about to fling towards him
where he sits tonight at the table where I am writing,
at the elbow of you who read.

SLEEPER

Your eyelid opens as you sleep,
gleam of white marble underneath
hinting your blindness to the day,
and fascination with the forms
which I assume your mind projects
within the upturned eye.

Imagining a dream for you
I fill the dubious abyss
which opens, if I should suppose
that nothing fills your mind, that 'now'
for you is not, was not, will never be

and our simultaneity,
our now and here this Sunday morning
only a fiction I propose
which founders in nonentity
if it attempts to pass the gates of sleep,

blank marble, where the dreamless one
(which will be you) plays truant still
from name, and time, and sex, and all,
and you and I have never met
until you wake,
or turn to dream again.

PERPLEXED BY THE SUNLIGHT

The boy is perplexed by the sunlight:
after four days of sheltering
underground, outside the village,
he wanders homeward, to meet
chaos: the dead cattle, voices chattering,
the first fires being relit after the barrage.

Turning slowly above the delta,
the pilot edges over the green map
his silver triangle. Perplexed by the sunlight,
he only half-attends to the navigator,
is half-surprised to feel the cargo drop
and plane leap sunward; he cannot see the target.

A FALLING HOUSE

I have wandered all night long
through the great chaotic house
and pushed my way through the throng
of terrible strangers, their words
hoarding a panic worse because the sense
lies always just out of reach
where mind gropes but cannot touch:

a deranged nobleman, cobweb-fingered
among his heavy-jewelled rings;
a psychopathic boy, who left
a dead child at the stair-foot
(there was a nurse who fainted at the sight);
old men, friendly, coaxing as reptiles;
old women, toothless, lewd as whores.

All night I fought to keep my breath
amid the fetid vacuum of these other
selves, and today I see
how nearly I am of their kind—
king who sits among conspirators—
and know that one day, one of them
may come to sit in the chair of my mind.

COLOUR WORDS

We have as many colours as we need:
Homer compared the dark sea to dark wine,
careless of other tints, and satisfied
with dark and light to pattern his design.

The Saxons felt as one the surface-tone
texture and colour gave to hand and eye,
summing in *bryn* the glint of steel or stone,
in *glæs* the blue-green-grey of lake or sky.

The merchant-hand divided red from gold,
piling its coloured cargoes in between:
bringing the concept 'orange' into hold,
and, later, the more subtle 'tangerine'.

Advances in industrial chemistry
offered themselves to painters, who began
to educate sensations of the eye
into chrome yellow and viridian.

Now 'Alkyd Gloss' and Polyurethane
tender their lush cosmetics to the sight.
Our rooms can dress themselves in 'forest green',
'candy' or 'eau-de-nil' or 'brilliant white',

'matador', 'golden willow', 'signal red'—
the names are gone before the paints are dry,
or patent words would talk the spectrum dead,
make Babel in the language of the eye.

INTERFACE

Turning the world upside down
I float like the four points of the compass
intersecting a flat ocean.
The world is weightless below me,
annihilated with a lungful of air:
Atlas the airborne clown on his back
with the world blown up like a bladder.

Weightlessness is my element.
The water isn't flat, it has its contours,
shaped to my body, the sea
inside me and out, adjusting its densities,
balancing my body against the mass,
the red and the green,
matter adjusting its destinies,

and I wonder why I stopped here
in my ride before birth through the zodiac of creatures,
why I was flung from the wheel
just thus, so that the spirals
of carbon stars within the cell
gelled to a constellation
this shape, and I was man?

Any other life would have been as easy.
Pitched here between air and water
I come to rest from the kingdom of earth
at the interface where the dolphins
surge up to breathe, who imagine the land is paradise,
who scatter the surface of the map, then dive
with my weight and the planet's on their backs.

CONDEMNED HOUSES

The tattooist's nervous customers
descend the basement steps
to meet their high priest of the skin
and consecrate imperfect bodies.
When they rejoin the street
their eyes are eager, with longing
to cry out how they have been changed
to dragons and swallows.

Their footsteps echo from the board-
blinded walls their symbols
will outlive.
            A stony garden
shrugging its slow walls, that yield
to the tenacious
grassblade, remembers
amongst the vagueness one explicit path
where cats will stroll in sunshine,
or, in sovereignty, stretch;

and one disastrous rose-tree, question-
crooked, whose tattered blooms
are gathered by a girl who takes them
to the flat downstairs.

Etched on the memory, these things
may survive a little while,
isolated as the tattooist's
skin-discarded fancies.

A few months more, the broken houses
shed continuous echoes
into time.

OPHELIA AT HER MIRROR, UNDECIDED

        But shall I fall sinking softly below
       into the arms of my cold lover, deep in
   my own death, taking another life, restful and strong,
     (in revenge) a doom that will harm them most
  that others cannot cure and lose among lilies
my stony bridegroom and my mind, cold
    with his coldness like a sharp spear of ice
       freeze myself to break at last;
 in one harsh kiss that the water will give me
     my love will turn its new passion
          to hatred unhuman and best
         in an instant my hair will tangle
       with reeds for my only mourners, reeds, my
          bridal veil pillow and deathbed alike
           I cannot I shall

DICTIONARY

Weighing perhaps ten pounds, it makes the desk
an altar. Other books and casual objects
   congregate themselves around it.

It is a god: I can place anything,
whether a grand piano or a microscope
   beside it, sure without checking

that inside those black covers it is named.
I can perform no action which this oracle
   cannot define and number

and ratify by quoted precedent.
I imagine the books on my shelves feeling humbled:
   it swallowed them all before they existed,

its belly contains infinite others like them.
Only by gibberish could they escape,
   and scarcely then: it defines *Jabberwock*,

and *gobbledeygook* (substantive, US slang)
and knows who coined the words, which it takes as tribute.
   It is alpha and omega.

Where shall we go to escape the eye of the god
which is Word? Into our dreams, perhaps,
   the love and confusion we can't express,

for if we say them the book will swallow them
as (and here I feel a certain frustration)
   it has already swallowed this poem,

motionless and emotionless as God.
I struggle to breathe parts of it into life.
   The dumb, idiot book says nothing.

THE HOROSCOPE

The necklace is unstrung:
you turn the planets over in your fingers
like gold beads, feeling each one
as if you recall the facets, the aspects
by memory of touch,
choosing a place in the circle
for weight and consequence of each.

This is deciphering,
a patient paleography of sky
where all the shattered text
is joined. And random stars that shook like dice
out from the cup of birth, assigned
their places in the song, relearn
the ordered numbers of the mind.

Knowledge or metaphor,
your art of understanding and the music
of planets call my scepticism
into the dance. We spin in the same house,
look: the moment is propitious.
Join up the broken constellations,
accept my stars, put on the necklace.

MIRRORS

We have cultivated new souls for ourselves
and set them to swim in pools of glass and mercury.
Like us, they are fragile, articulate,

shallower than the pupil of an eye,
always rather pale, rather nervous,
always a hair out of place, a smile not quite moulded.

The Greeks had mirrors of bronze, which may have been
kinder: even the closest scrutiny
would evoke only a warm, approximate image

and carry it without risk of breakage,
of carpets spined with anger or clumsiness,
the stress our poor cold shadows can't endure.

But we must consult the omens with mathematical
exactness, demand unglazed facts from faces
sanctified with mineral pallor,

preferring the truth cool and without colour
but sharp enough still to set self-doubt flowing
like blood sometimes, and fetch the hungry ghosts.

PLAYING THE FRUIT-MACHINE

Locked in, I look for the combination
that'll set something free.
Hand to hand with this machine,
this coin-junkie I fix with money,
chrome hustler with one stiff arm,
sometimes I think I'm standing in front of a mirror:

the tumblers spin, cherries and bells
thud and smile at the windows of my heart,
no one looks out. The signs
are out of line again,
nothing will be revealed. This machine
has a block against giving;

I'm hooked on solving a problem for a sym-
biotic siamese twin,
and the needle's jammed in the vein,
the chromium thickens into my blood
with a sharp tarnish like the flavour of hands
sour with fumbling money.

THE VAMPIRE'S CONFESSION

I think I can never have enough
of words and kisses and tears;
my lips are heavy with the richness
as I lie and dream in my red dark.

I'll call you up some time on the telephone
to feel you lift my cupped voice to your cheek:
a thin, scraped voice with a lick of love
to nuzzle your ear like a little black tongue.

Invite me round and I'll turn to a babe in your arms,
bald and white-faced with crying.
I'll sing you into a trance with my problems,
bed down with you on my prickly anxieties,

talking, not talking; sleeping, not sleeping.
In the morning, you know, I'm tired with the effort
but I have my colour back and yours too.
I often walk home with the white stars of morning

on the clean pavements. I feel like a fed child,
my lips pout with strawberry paint.
I could get through a good many days alone
after a night with you.

I should turn your smallest attentions over
and over in the dark to learn their shapes,
and try how your comforts would taste in my mouth
and examine your various echoes.

In short, I confess (I love confessing)
I'd steal your time, your words, your gestures
and leave you with absences, headaches, a suspicion
that your own needs betrayed you into mine.

SADE IN PRISON

He dreamt about this bottle: if you drew
the cork, or broke its neck,
a flood would gush out big enough to drown
the Bastille, or wreck a city;
yet it lay with the debris under a table.

The dream recurred, and he needed it,
so carefully refrained
from telling anyone. Like a moth
put in a flask and buried,
it fluttered from time to time underground.

And watching at his window—human scum
that swilled about the streets
cursing, unreflective, in love with filth—
why not just let it loose,
once having got your hands on the sluice-gates?

If you could find the way. (His world defined
by stone and mortar
so his head sometimes seemed to pack the room,
he saw everyone jammed
down with a cork. Freedom is breaking out.)

Energy is destruction. He compiled
books to put his case:
You, fools, at least destroy your inhibitions—
for everybody, copulation
of some kind, somehow, might set something loose;

and once loose—well, let that come later.
It finds its own direction.
Sade, thrown to his feet by revolution,
lost all his taste for death
or individual murder, gulped in the flood, and sank

to scratch himself, years later, at Charenton
wondering why law came back,
why energy was put in an asylum,
offered its share of straw and chains
not to suggest the presence of some lack

in sound Napoleonic prosperity.
And he went mad that way:
walled in, his only solace that old bottle
between his thighs
which he uncorked a dozen times a day.

THE ISLAND

When I came to the island
I knew the maps were wrong—
there were rocks where there were no rocks,
and the cherubs blew back-to-front winds,
puffing their cheeks with fictions
against the gales of that land.
I sailed in a fog of truths become lies
in transport from the old countries,
a madness of false projections.
Only quadrant and star
were real, and the glimpse of moon-white water
to give a warning of reefs.
Here you bring nothing with you, said the island.

In the morning I discarded the maps
and the old inks ran in the salt water,
the trade routes blossomed, continents
floated out on the ocean currents.
The sun dried my clothes,
the sand was real under my feet.
I am this, the island said.

MOVING

You had your time, and there it goes:
the poems are your calendar,
the chronicle you made, the rows
of pictograms left when your tribe moved on,
news for the archaeologist alone
whose scholarship will falsify your culture.

Your astrology becomes illegible:
already there's change in your fixed stars,
stones are displaced, untraceable
all the mythologies you partly lived in,
from Sweet Melinda to the Acid Queen;
no trace of your belief in life on Mars.

The bulldozers approach to raze
the settlements you held,
the dark rooms with their heaped ashtrays,
the starving meters you fed for heat,
the arguments, the typing late at night,
the awkward poems that refused to yield.

What it means now is anyone's guess.
And guessed wrong, if anyone believe
merely what the words express.
Only the gaps in your incomplete
archives suggest the things that wouldn't fit,
the ones you carry with you as you leave.